A Slice of Mud Pie

by Stephanie Herbek   illustrated by Ashley Mims

Scott Foresman
is an imprint of

PEARSON

Glenview, Illinois • Boston, Massachusetts • Chandler, Arizona
Upper Saddle River, New Jersey

Illustrations
Ashley Mims

Photographs
Every effort has been made to secure permission and provide appropriate credit for photographic material. The publisher deeply regrets any omission and pledges to correct errors called to its attention in subsequent editions.

Unless otherwise acknowledged, all photographs are the property of Pearson Education, Inc.

12 ©Peter Anderson/Getty Images

ISBN 13: 978-0-328-50853-2
ISBN 10:   0-328-50853-5

9 10 V010 13

"Pie?" asked Charlie as he walked into Mr. Fernando's classroom. "Why are we studying pie today?"

"I love pie!" cheered Will. "That sounds great!"

"Good morning!" said Mr. Fernando. He walked into the room holding a box. "As part of our soil unit, we'll be looking at *mud* pies today. Grab some pie, but watch out for worms!"

"Worms?" Meg and Emily gasped.
"*Mud* pie?" growled Will. "I like my pie to have apples, not worms! I like it to be smooth, not full of dirt!"

"Will, I'm glad you said that," said Mr. Fernando. "If your favorite pie has a smooth texture, it must have small particles. The soil I used to make this mud pie is made up of large particles. Those particles gave the pie its texture."

"It's not smooth at all," Will said.

Mr. Fernando unrolled a large picture of mud pie.

"Let's look at this chart," he said. "This mud pie is made of substances from nature. Rocks, dirt, and sand are parts of the soil. Soil makes up this mud pie."

TOP

Dirt
Sand
Rock

SIDE

The students looked at their own pieces of mud pie.

"What other things are in the soil?" asked Mr. Fernando.

"I see worms in my soil," answered Meg.

"Worms make sure the soil has air," said Mr. Fernando.

"Now let's talk about soil," Mr. Fernando said. He started to write on the board. "Soil is made up of four materials. It has sand grains, air, water, and something called *humus*."

"Aren't sand grains just small particles of rock?" asked Emily.

"That's right," said Mr. Fernando with a smile. "You really know your soil!"

Soil is:
1. sand grains
2. air
3. water
4. humus

"Why does soil have air?" asked Charlie.

"Rain is full of substances that help plants grow," answered Mr. Fernando. "Air spaces let rain seep into the soil. The water goes down to the roots of a plant below the ground. Then the plant sucks up the water. Worms help the soil have air."

"What is humus?" asked Will.

"Humus is little pieces of dead animals and plants. It makes the soil look black or brown," explained Mr. Fernando.

"Yuck!" said Will with a frown. "I think humus is gross!"

10

RRRRRRING! The school bell jingled.

"It's time for lunch!" called Mr. Fernando. "We'll finish the rest of our lesson later."

"We learned all about soil. What's left?" asked Will.

"Worms!" Mr. Fernando grinned. "Enjoy your lunch!"

Worms Help the Earth

Worms live in soil all over the world. If soil has enough food and water, worms can live in it. Most worms live near the top of the soil. They eat dead plants and animals, soil, and tiny rocks.

Worms help the earth in many ways. Worms are food for hungry animals and birds. Worms also help plants. When worms wiggle through soil, they help air get in. Worms also make tunnels that help water drain from the soil. Worms help make the soil rich and good for growing plants. Farmers love worms because worms help their crops grow.

Earthworms